BORN OF FIRE
The Volcanic Origin of
Yellowstone National Park

An imaginary view of the caldera as it might have appeared 600,000 years ago to a park visitor who hiked up Mt. Washburn for a view.

BORN OF FIRE

The Volcanic Origin of Yellowstone National Park

Dr. William H. Cottrell

Roberts Rinehart, Inc. Publishers
in cooperation with the Yellowstone Association
for Natural Science, History and Education

This book is dedicated to Carol, Will, and Zach, my wife and sons, who patiently endured the painstakingly slow process of distillation.

© Copyright 1987 William H. Cottrell, Jr.
Published by Roberts Rinehart, Inc. Publishers
P.O. Box 3161, Boulder, Colorado 80303
International Standard Book Number 0-911797-35-1
Library of Congress Catalog Card Number 87-61259
Design and Production by Dave Comstock

CONTENTS

ACKNOWLEDGMENTS

In the fast-paced 1980s there are those persons who still manage to squeeze a little more into their day's work. I would especially like to acknowledge those generous individuals who gave their valuable time to assist this project to completion. Their admirable tolerance of my geologic naivete provided a positive atmosphere for asking questions and obtaining answers. In short, they were all great to work with.

Interpretive Rangers Gary and Rebecca Davies, Roger Anderson and Dan Ng reviewed my rough drafts and said there was indeed a space on the shelves for this kind of book. George Robinson, Chief of Interpretation, was incredibly positive, encouraging, and always had time for a phone call. Rick Rinehart outlined the problems of the publishing world. Wayne Hamilton, Chief Geologist at Yellowstone, patiently corrected my geological misconceptions and urged me to scientific accuracy. Timothy Manns, North District Naturalist, and Peter Allen, Interpretive Ranger, smoothed off the rough edges and made sure the park visitor would get clear and accurate information. David Comstock faithfully reproduced the manuscript and designed the pages to gain maximum communication potential.

For financial assistance I express my gratitude to Dr. and Mrs. William H. Cottrell, Sr. of Kansas City, and Mr. and Mrs. Z. K. Brinkerhoff of Denver.

PREFACE

This book was purposefully designed for readers who are curious about the geological formation of Yellowstone Park, but who have limited vacation time to spend interpreting the technical language common to so many geology books.

The author applies recent concepts and theories of earth science to Yellowstone Park while omitting time scales and technical language. Millions of years compress into an hour of reading; just right for passing the time waiting for Old Faithful geyser to erupt.

The book provides a very basic understanding of the surprisingly active earth's crust and the geological curiosities called hot spots. It then shows how crust and hot spot interaction volcanically produced Yellowstone Park. For the vacationing non-geologist, this is the ultimate geological short story.

W. H. C.

"Simplify, simplify, simplify. . . ."—H. D. Thoreau.

I. STRUCTURE OF THE EARTH

The surface of the earth changes constantly. Continents drift on a sea of melted rock, like ice floes on the ocean. Mountains rise and fall as the drifting continents bend and fold during collisions with each other. Liquid rock pours out on the earth's surface through volcanoes and cracks called rifts. New earth crust formation balances crust destruction. These processes occur over millions of years, and until recently defied human appreciation. Now the earth's surface may be viewed as a structure that slowly but continuously changes.

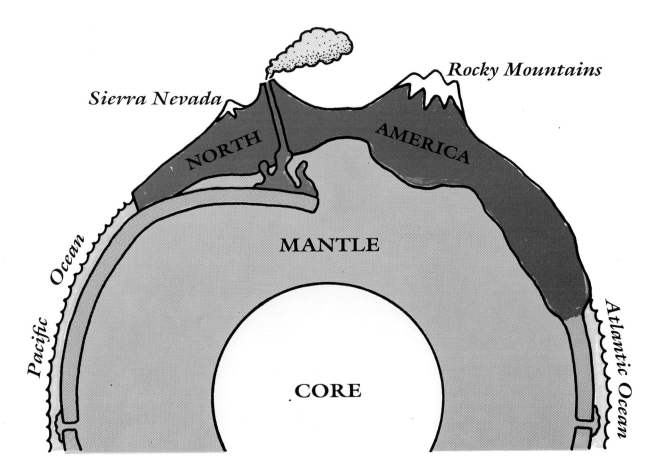

A cross section of the earth reveals a **core**, **mantle**, and **crust**. The cooled solidified crust floats on the very hot semiliquid **mantle layer**, much like sheets of ice float on a partially frozen pond. The ice is not attached to the water and drifts on the pond according to forces of wind and current.

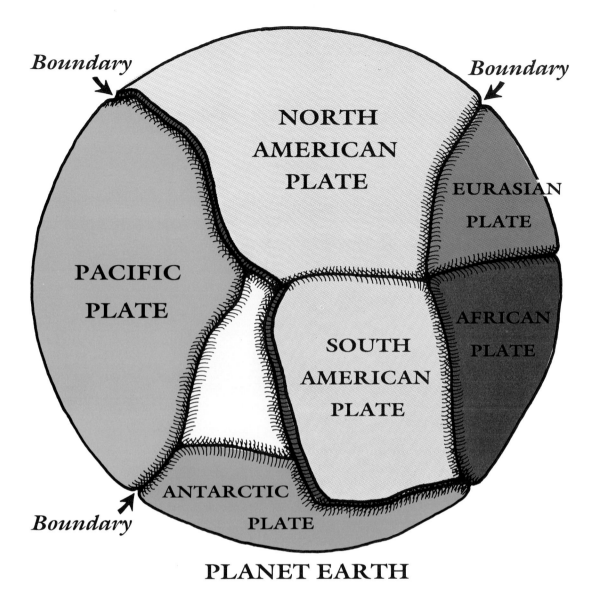

Boundary

NORTH
AMERICAN
PLATE

Boundary

EURASIAN
PLATE

PACIFIC
PLATE

AFRICAN
PLATE

SOUTH
AMERICAN
PLATE

Boundary

ANTARCTIC
PLATE

PLANET EARTH

    The crust layer of the earth is subdivided into large pieces called **plates**. These gigantic plates drift about the surface of the planet. Plates meet and interact at their boundaries. Sometimes they scrape, sometimes they override one another, and sometimes they collide head-on. The physical interactions of plates at their boundaries produce dramatic changes in the landscape such as mountain ranges, volcanoes, and earthquakes. The main force that imparts motion to the plates is probably **convection**.

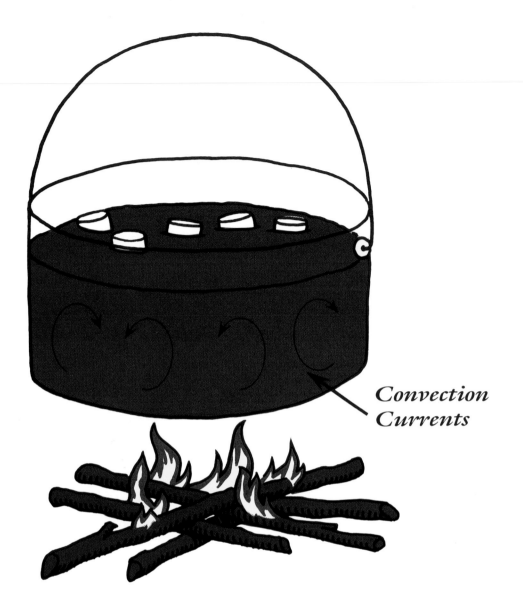

Convection
Currents

The force of **convection** is demonstrated by a pot of slowly heating cocoa drink with marshmallows floating on top. Heat warms the bottom layer, which rises to trade places with the top layer, which sinks to the bottom where it is then heated. This cycle of rising and falling according to temperature is called convection. **Convection currents** stir the cocoa and move the marshmallows about on its surface.

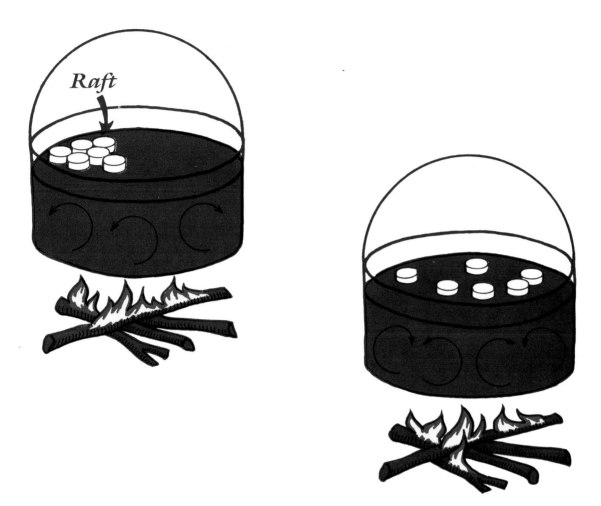

Convection currents may drive the marshmallows together to form a raft. The same currents then well up under the raft and break it apart. Convection currents in the **mantle layer** of the earth appear to push **plates** together and break them apart in a similar manner.

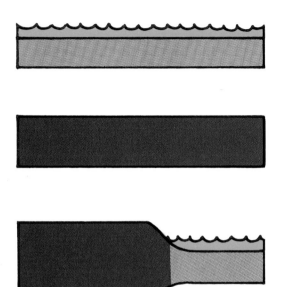

Oceanic Crust

Continental Crust

Combination of Oceanic and Continental Crust

The drifting plates of crust vary in composition, for there are two different types of crust: **oceanic crust** is thinner but heavier, and underlies the oceans; **continental crust** is thicker but lighter, and forms the dry land of the continents.

Most plates are made of a combination of continental and oceanic crust and bear names like the **North American plate**, the **South American plate**, or the **African plate**. Plates underlying the ocean are composed of oceanic crust.

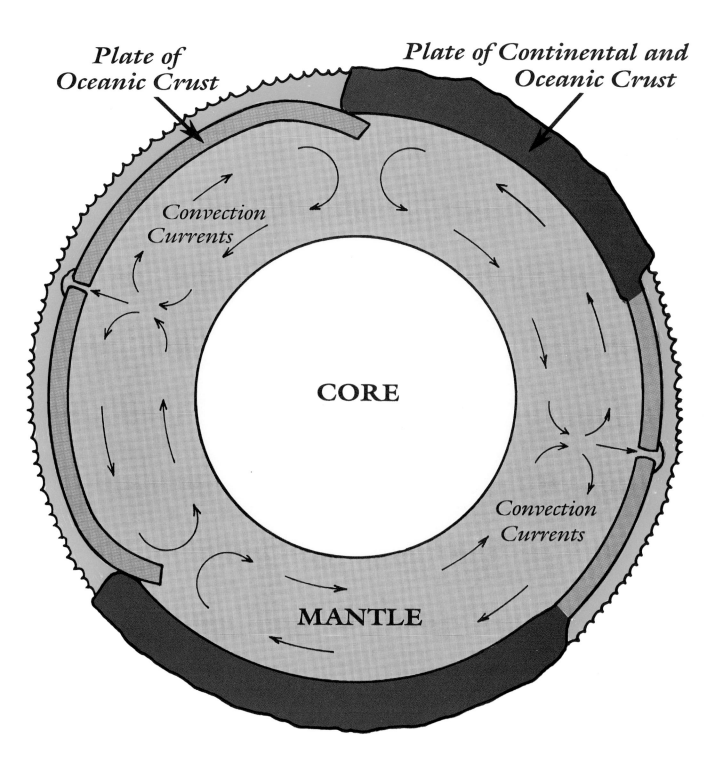

Plate of
Oceanic Crust

Plate of Continental and
Oceanic Crust

Convection
Currents

Convection
Currents

CORE

MANTLE

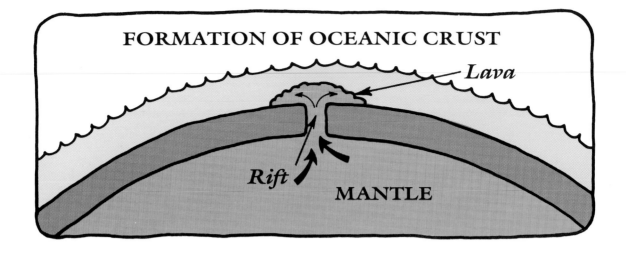

FORMATION OF OCEANIC CRUST

Lava

Rift

MANTLE

Plates of crust are created and destroyed in a recycling process. Melted rock called **lava** pours out of cracks or **rifts** in the crust to form new **oceanic crust**. This process forces the two plates of oceanic crust apart and results in **sea-floor spreading**.

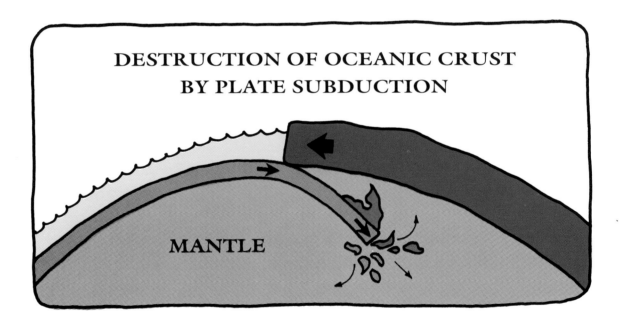

**DESTRUCTION OF OCEANIC CRUST
BY PLATE SUBDUCTION**

MANTLE

A plate of thin, cold, dense **oceanic crust** is forced back into the mantle by the overriding thicker, lighter **continental crust** of another plate. The descending oceanic crust will remelt and recycle. The process where one plate goes under another is **subduction**. The lighter continental crust **overrides** the descending oceanic crust.

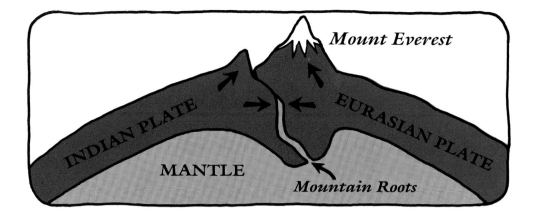

Sometimes plates of continental crust **collide** and neither plate will return to the mantle, but rise high in the air, forming the great mountain ranges. **Roots** of these mountains extend deep into the mantle layer.

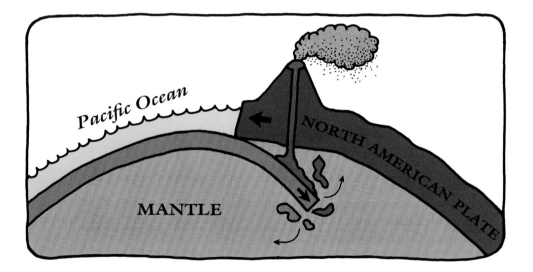

Where continental plates override oceanic plates, intense **earthquake activity** accompanies the scraping of the two plates and the breaking up of the descending oceanic plate. The descending plate remelts and new lighter **magma** rises up under the overriding plate and melts through the crust to form volcanoes. The west coasts of North, Central, and South America vividly demonstrate volcanic mountain ranges formed by plate collision and overriding. The first period of volcanic activity in the Yellowstone region was probably due to the **North American plate** overriding the **Pacific oceanic plates**, with the subsequent associated volcanism.

GENERAL CYCLE OF PLATE FORMATION AND

Mount Fuji ③ *Pacific Ocean Plate*
Japan ① ④ *Pacific Rift*

Eurasian Plate

MANTLE

① Pacific Ocean plates sink beneath and **recycle** under the Eurasian and Philippine plates to the west.

② Pacific Ocean plates sink beneath the **overriding** American plates along the western coastlines of North, Central, and South America.

③ The destroyed crust recycles through **volcanoes**, and

④ returns to the surface at **Mid-Pacific Ocean rifts** to form new oceanic crust.

DESTRUCTION IN THE WESTERN HEMISPHERE

Mount St. Helens ③

Rocky Mountains

Appalachian Mountains

Mid-Atlantic Rift ⑤

North American Plate

MANTLE

The North American plate **moves westward** over the Pacific Ocean plates.

⑤ The **Mid-Atlantic rift** forms new North American plate crust and pushes the plate westward. Generally, continental crust is rarely destroyed and oceanic crust is frequently destroyed. The width of the Pacific Ocean floor **lessens** yearly due to plate destruction along its eastern and western borders. The Atlantic sea floor **spreads** wider each year.

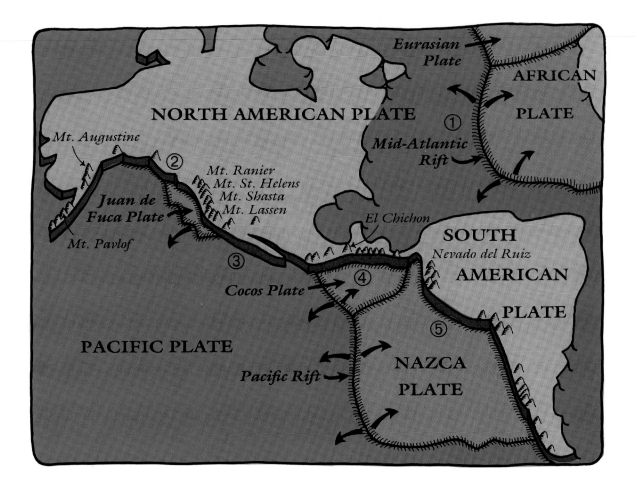

The western coastline of the American continents presents a complicated picture of interacting continental and oceanic plates. Several observations about plate interaction are noted:

① The American plates originate from the **Mid-Atlantic rift.**
② The North American plate overrides the descending **Juan de Fuca plate.**
③ The California coast scrapes but does not override the Pacific plate.
④ Central America overrides the descending **Cocos plate.**
⑤ South America overrides the descending **Nazca plate**.

When plates override one another, earthquakes and volcanoes commonly occur, as the western coast of the Americas demonstrates.

To appreciate the relationship of drifting continental plates to Yellowstone Park it is necessary to examine the origin of modern continental plates. At one very ancient time all of the earth's continental crust was fused into a single **supercontinent** named Pangaea, which means "all land."

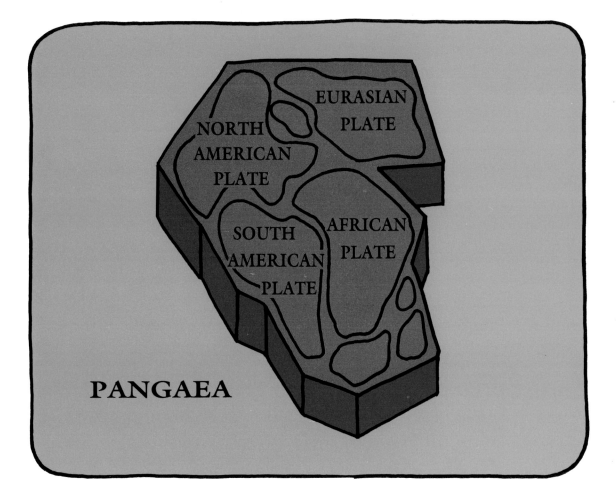

PANGAEA

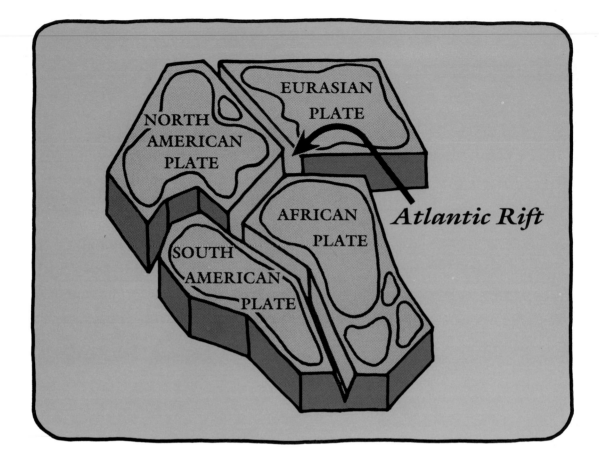

Convection currents in the earth's mantle boiled up beneath Pangaea and broke it into several smaller continental plates. A large crack called the **Mid-Atlantic rift** divided Pangaea into the North American, South American, African, and Eurasian plates. Sea water gradually filled the ever-widening rift between the continents and formed the **Atlantic Ocean**.

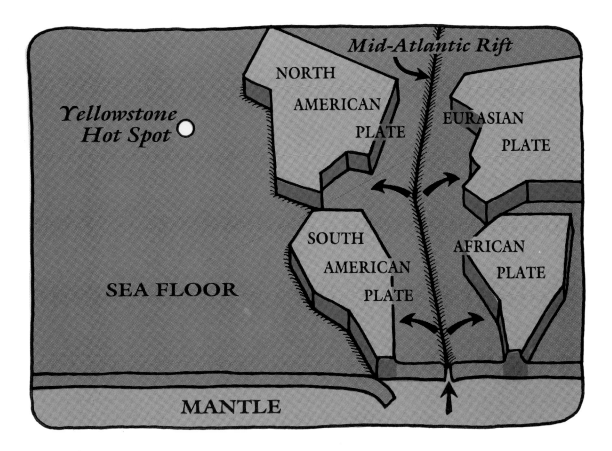

New **magma** from the mantle layer poured into the Mid-Atlantic rift, thereby creating new oceanic crust and a spreading sea floor. The Atlantic Ocean **widened**, as did the distance between the continents.

The North American plate drifted westward toward a unique geological feature called a **hot spot**. This hot spot would eventually provide energy to Yellowstone Park, but not until the drifting North American plate overrode it.

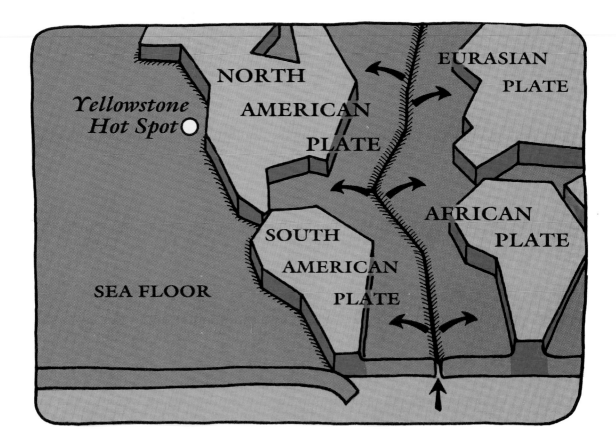

The spreading sea floor pushed the North American plate westward until it encountered the **Yellowstone Hot Spot** along the northern coast of California. The North American plate then moved onto the hot spot by overriding it.

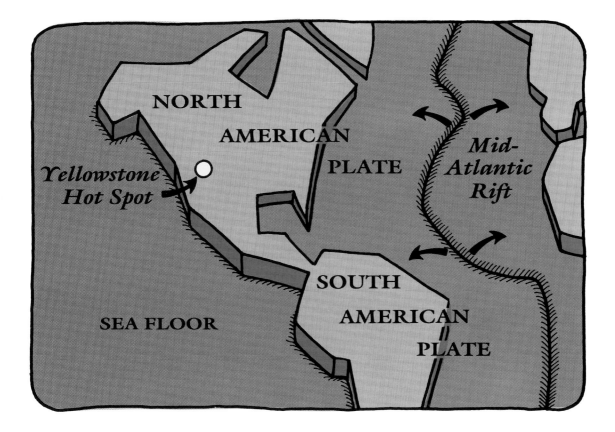

The hot spot **melted holes** in the underside of the continental crust from the California coast to Wyoming, leaving a trail of **volcanic signs** such as Craters of the Moon National Monument. The continent continued its westward movement over the hot spot until that portion of the North American plate now called Yellowstone National Park came to rest over the hot spot.

II. HOT SPOTS

Hot spots provide the energy for formation and maintenance of the park's **geothermal** features ("geo" means earth and "thermal" refers to heat). Yellowstone country contains many geothermal features: geysers, hot springs, mud pots, and fumeroles.

The earth's crust under Yellowstone lies over a hot spot. A metal plate passed slowly over a blow torch would leave a trail of burnt spots on its undersurface. When the continental plate drifts slowly over a hot spot, this heat source leaves a trail of volcanic activity where it melts into the plate passing over it.

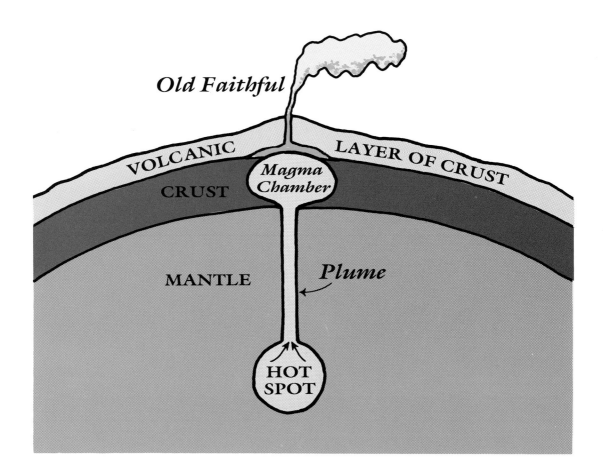

HOT SPOT UNDER OCEANIC PLATES

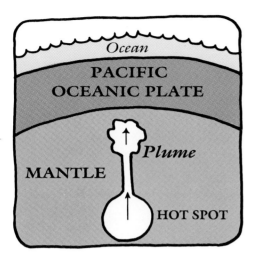

A geological hot spot is a source of tremendous geothermal heat **anchored immovably** in the deep mantle layer. The heat of the hot spot forms a rising column or **plume** of melted rock which ascends through the mantle to the undersurface of the earth's crust.

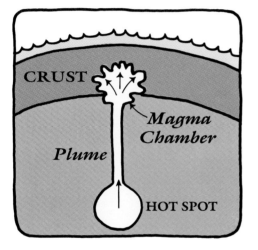

The plume of **magma** melts into the crust and forms a **magma chamber,** or reservoir. The plume acts like a pipe delivering magma to the crust.

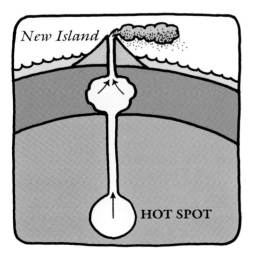

When the magma melts through the **oceanic crust**, it forms volcanoes which become mountain islands like Hawaii.

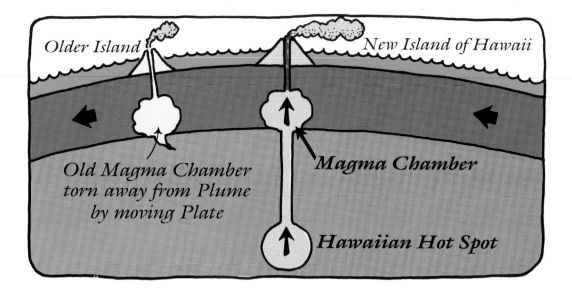

As the Pacific plate continues its westward drift over the immovable hot spot, older magma chambers **break away** from the plume and new ones form. Each new hot spot magma chamber may form a **volcanic island** (arrows in the crust indicate direction of plate movement).

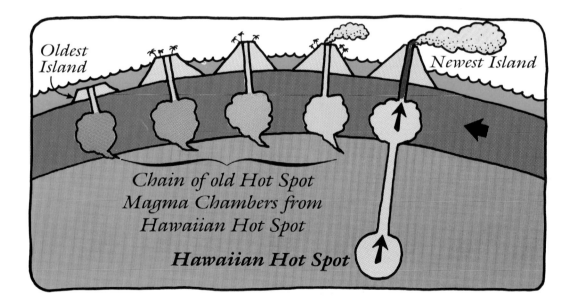

The Hawaiian hot spot formed a chain of volcanic islands thousands of miles long as it melted a trail into the drifting Pacific Ocean plate.

HOT SPOT UNDER CONTINENTAL PLATES

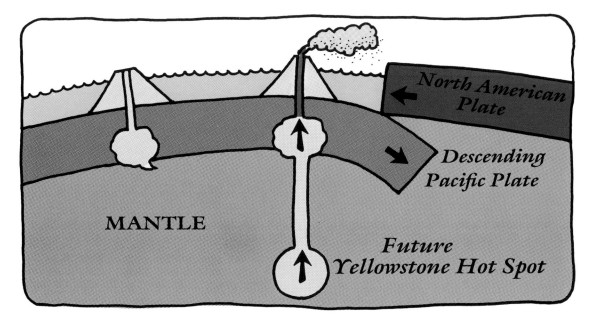

Pacific oceanic crust once may have covered the future Yellowstone hot spot.

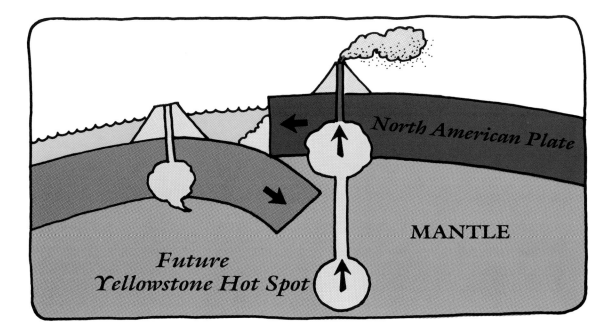

The westward drifting North American plate overrode the hot spot at the northern California coast. The hot spot then melted holes in the continental crust of North America.

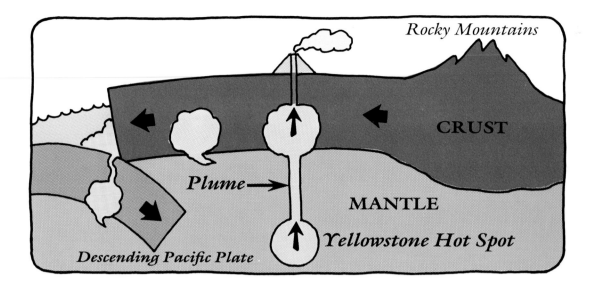

The plate drifted westward over the hot spot, which left a trail of volcanic signs across the western United States. The Snake River plain and Craters of the Moon National Monument are examples.

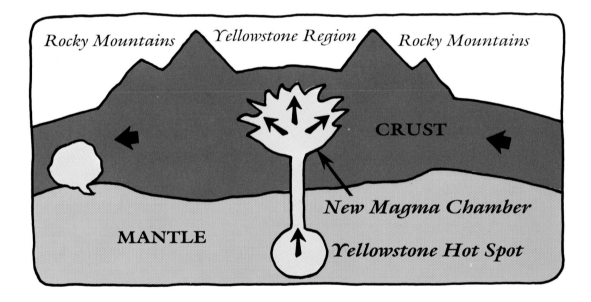

The region of the North American plate known today as Yellowstone Park moved onto the hot spot. The **hot spot plume** melted into the crust beneath Yellowstone and formed a large **magma chamber** which provided the geothermal energy for **volcanism**.

III. VOLCANIC ORIGIN OF YELLOWSTONE PARK

The previous sections provided geological concepts useful to understanding the volcanic origin of the park. The actual physical construction of the landscape by the earth required violent volcanoes, mud and lava flows, glaciers, earthquakes and cataclysmic movement of many cubic miles of rock.

There were two major periods of volcanic activity that formed modern Yellowstone Park. The first came about when the North American plate buckled and cracked, giving rise to the Rocky Mountains. Volcanic activity was caused by the North American plate overriding a Pacific Ocean plate.

The second period of volcanic activity occurred when the region of Yellowstone came to rest over a hot spot. Volcanism from this hot spot produced much of Yellowstone's present landscape.

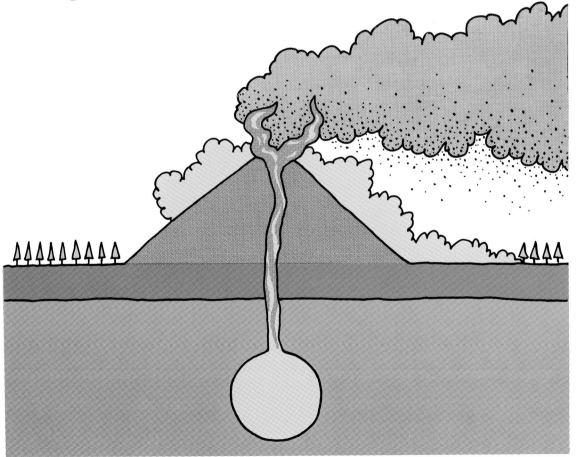

FIRST PERIOD OF VOLCANISM

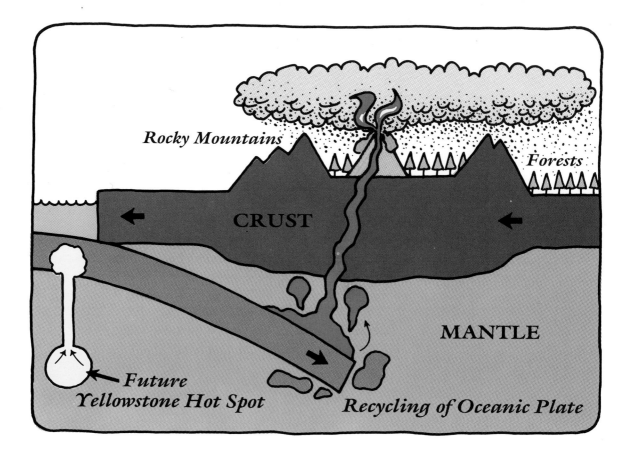

Rocky Mountains

Forests

CRUST

MANTLE

Future Yellowstone Hot Spot

Recycling of Oceanic Plate

When the North American plate overrode the Pacific Ocean plate the continent buckled, cracked, and created the Rocky Mountains. The descending oceanic plate broke up and melted. The recycled magma rose to the surface through weaknesses in the crust, forming volcanic mountain ranges.

Thick layers of volcanic material and avalanches of mud, sand, and rock buried many different forests. The Washburn and Absaroka mountain ranges and the petrified forests of Yellowstone are ancient remnants of the **First Period of Volcanism** that created the park. The hot spot destined for Yellowstone still lay under the Pacific Ocean plate to the west.

SECOND PERIOD OF VOLCANISM

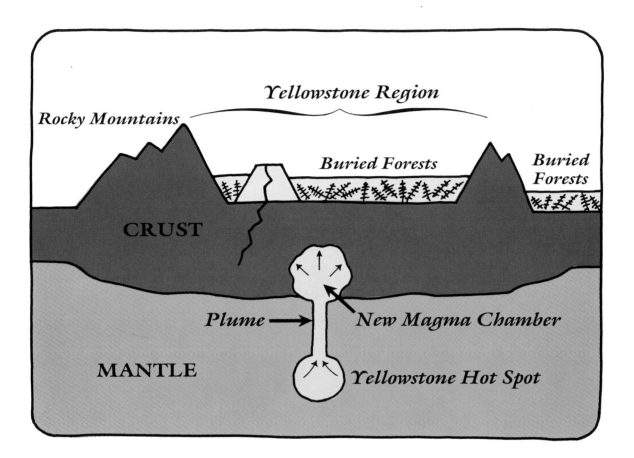

A long quiet period passed as the North American plate moved westward over the future hot spot of Yellowstone. When the Rocky Mountains of Wyoming moved onto the hot spot, the **Second Period of Volcanism** began.

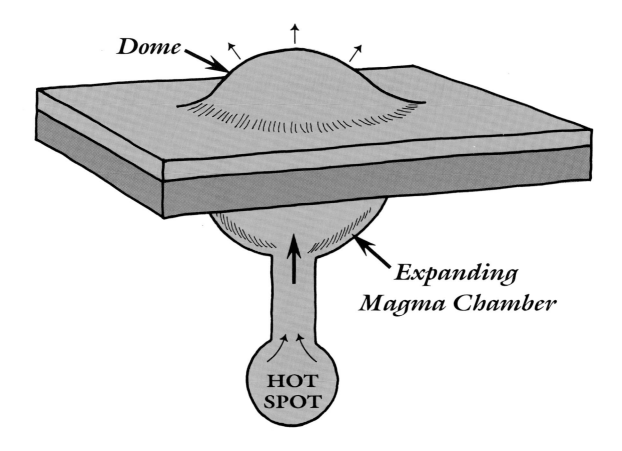

A **dome** appeared in the crust of the Yellowstone region when the Yellowstone hot spot created a new **magma chamber**. The expanding new magma chamber lifted the thin crust of the Yellowstone region.

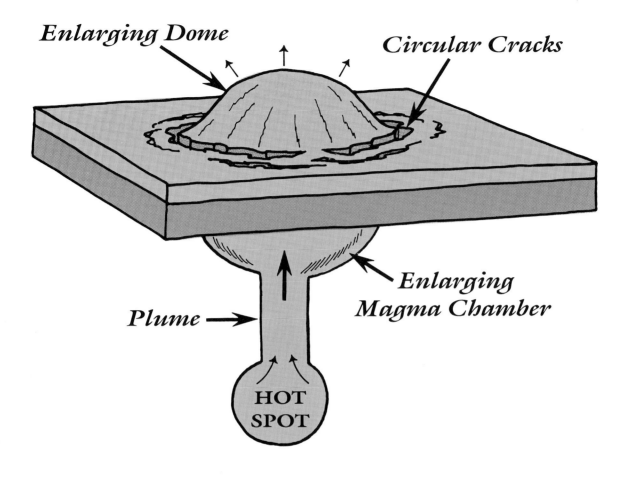

Enlarging Dome

Circular Cracks

Enlarging Magma Chamber

Plume

HOT SPOT

Circular cracks developed around the dome as the thin crust stretched and strained over the enlarging magma chamber. These cracks greatly weakened the crust that roofed the chamber.

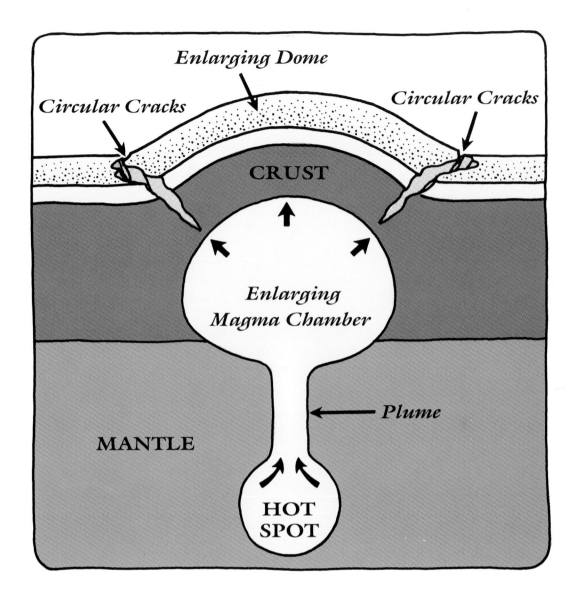

Enlarging Dome

Circular Cracks   *Circular Cracks*

CRUST

*Enlarging
Magma Chamber*

Plume

MANTLE

HOT
SPOT

Eventually the circular cracks in the crust met the
expanding and highly pressurized magma chamber.

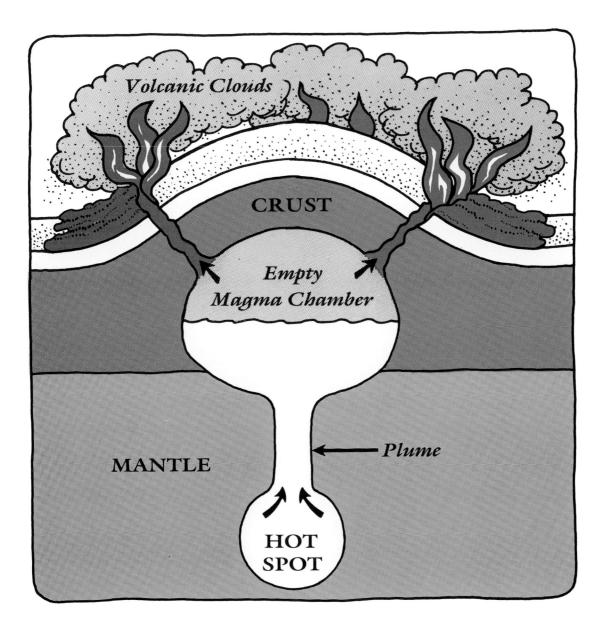

The pressurized magma burst from the cracks and spewed hundreds of cubic miles of volcanic **lava** and **ash** onto the Yellowstone region. The chamber was partially emptied, creating a structurally unsound roof over the chamber. This situation could exist only for a few seconds before the chamber roof collapsed.

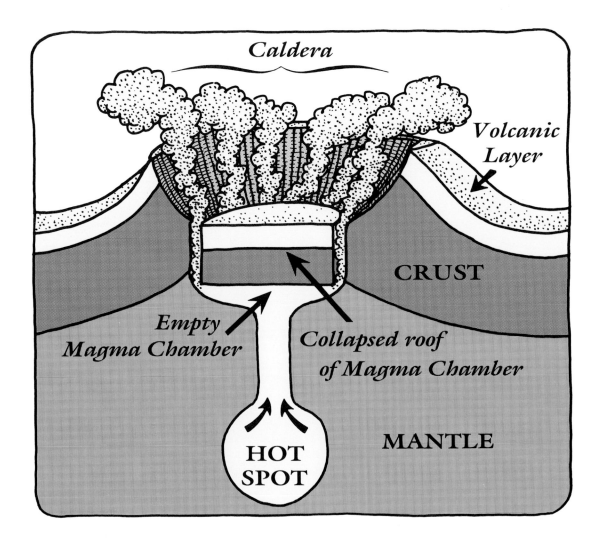

Caldera

Volcanic Layer

CRUST

Empty Magma Chamber

Collapsed roof of Magma Chamber

MANTLE

HOT SPOT

The immensely heavy roof collapsed suddenly and a 1000-square-mile section of Yellowstone plateau (the size of Rhode Island) sank, possibly several thousand feet. This collapse left a gigantic cup-shaped depression called a **caldera**, which means "hot basin." The eruption probably lasted days; the collapse took only hours.

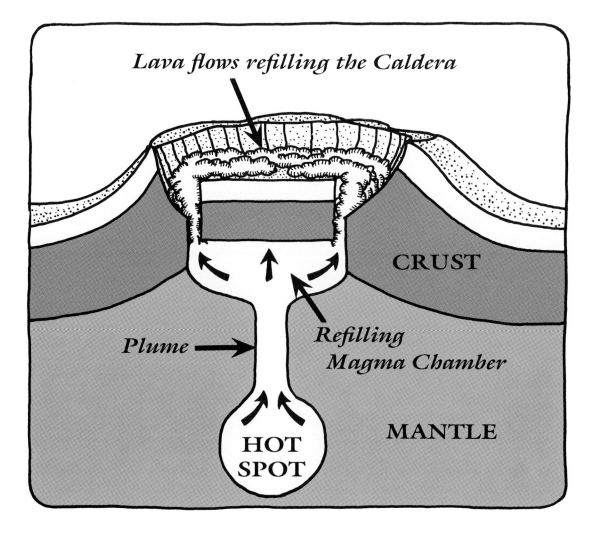

Lava flows refilling the Caldera

CRUST

Plume

Refilling Magma Chamber

MANTLE

HOT SPOT

The **caldera** floor flooded with **lava** to a depth of 1000 feet. The roof of the magma chamber (the floor of the caldera) was pushed upward by **refilling of the magma chamber**. Because these two processes raised the caldera floor and erosion lowered the rim around it, the Yellowstone caldera lacks the dramatic appearance of other volcanic calderas such as Crater Lake of Oregon, or Kilauea on the slopes of Mauna Loa in Hawaii Volcanoes National Park.

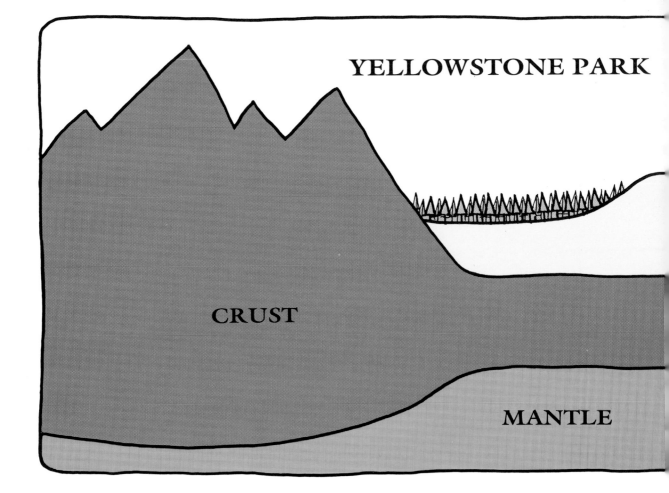

YELLOWSTONE PARK

CRUST

MANTLE

The giant caldera cooled. A portion of it collected water to form early **Lake Yellowstone**. Water penetrated deep into the permeable volcanic rock and was heated by the hot spot magma. The superheated waters returned to the surface in the form of **geysers** (Old Faithful), **mud pots, hot springs** and **fumeroles**. The Yellowstone, Madison, and Lewis rivers drain surface water from the caldera.

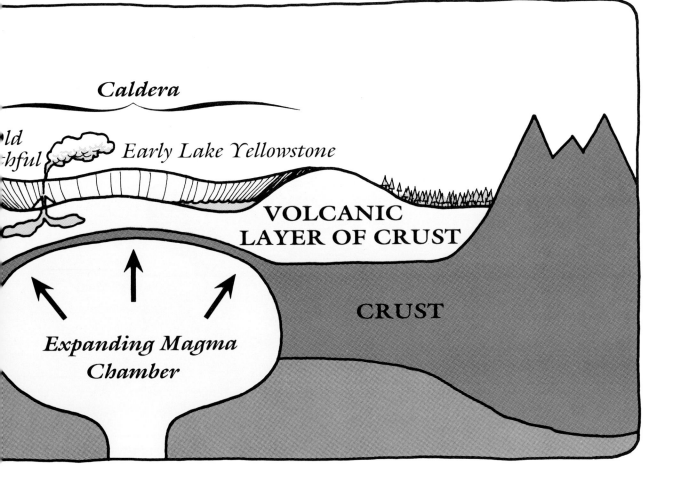

Caldera

*ld
hful*

Early Lake Yellowstone

**VOLCANIC
LAYER OF CRUST**

CRUST

*Expanding Magma
Chamber*

Yellowstone Park today is essentially an immense, shallow **caldera** in the center of a broad, flat plateau, surrounded on three sides by mountains. Glaciers and erosion over time finished the sculpture of Yellowstone Park, but volcanoes were the original artists of this unique place on earth.

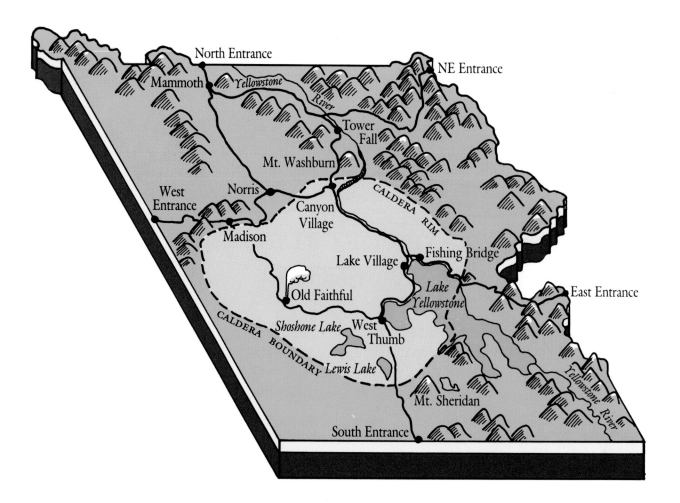

An exaggerated **overview** of Yellowstone Park demonstrates the large caldera occupying its central portion. If a road followed the rim it would be 140 miles long, as long as the Grand Loop Road which encircles the interior of the park.

Within the caldera the **geyser basins** of the Firehole River display their steamy beauty. **Lake Yellowstone** occupies the southwestern portion of the caldera and appears to overflow the rim. Actually, a rising caldera floor has caused the lake to backfill **old river canyons** that crossed the rim. Yellowstone River leaves the caldera at the northern rim.

IV. FUTURE, GUIDE, AND SUMMARY

This section explores the future possibility of volcanism in Yellowstone Park. Instructions for viewing the caldera from several points are followed by a page of numbers chronologically summarizing the major volcanic events, and a glossary concludes the section.

The floor of the caldera is **volcanically alive** and active. The magma chamber beneath the Yellowstone caldera is today pushing the floor upward an average of one inch yearly. The caldera floor is rising like bread in the oven. The crust cracks and slips, causing some of the numerous **earthquakes** recorded at Old Faithful Visitor Center. The growing dome in the caldera floor suggests that pressure builds daily underneath the thin crust of Yellowstone Park.

New cracks may develop in the bulging floor of the caldera, and earthquakes will rumble through the earth's crust. The weakened dome of the caldera floor will split open, permitting magma to flow again to the surface of Yellowstone. The new volcanic activity may be gentle, like the volcanoes of Hawaii, or as cataclysmic as Mount Saint Helens. Considering Yellowstone's past geological history, the more violent form of volcanism probably will reshape the Yellowstone plateau at some future time.

If volcanism similar to that of the past returns to Yellowstone Park, a large smoking caldera might occupy the plateau again.

GUIDE TO BEST VIEWS
OF THE CALDERA

Where to See the Caldera

The rim of the Yellowstone caldera is very difficult to appreciate; erosive forces of ice, snow, and rain have largely obliterated it. Lava flows gradually filled the caldera and overflowed it. But with a little imagination and instruction the general size of the immense caldera and its rim can be seen from Mount Washburn and Lake Butte.

How to See the Caldera

First, drive or hike to one of the viewpoints listed below. Then hold the appropriate panoramic diagram (pages 41-45) up to the horizon and match up the labeled landmarks. Once oriented in this fashion, one can pick out the approximate location of the caldera rim and appreciate the immensity of the Yellowstone caldera.

The 1987 Official Map and Guide to Yellowstone Park shows the caldera outline in excellent detail; it can be obtained from the visitor centers.

Mount Washburn Viewpoints

North of Canyon Village, Mt. Washburn overlooks the entire caldera and provides the most complete views. The road from Canyon to Tower ascends the slopes of Mt. Washburn, an ancient volcano. Three miles north of Canyon Junction, the Washburn Hot Springs Viewpoint provides a good but incomplete view of the caldera because it is 1500 feet lower than the Washburn summit.

The best view is obtained by driving five miles from Canyon Junction to Dunraven Pass parking area and then ascending the 3-mile trail to the summit. The Mt. Washburn Lookout Station Viewpoint is equipped with an enclosed viewing area, telescope and restrooms. The entire extent of the caldera can be appreciated best from this point on a clear day.

Be sure to check with the Visitor Center at Canyon Village before making the trip to get advice about weather, trail conditions, and appropriate clothing, food, and water to bring. Summer storms can be violent and occur on many afternoons. It's wise to plan ahead.

Lake Butte Viewpoint

Ten miles east of Lake Junction, a side road winds .9 mile up to Lake Butte Overlook, which offers spectacular views of Lake Yellowstone and much of the expanse of the caldera. It does not require a hike.

MOUNT WASHBURN LOOKOUT VIEWPOINT

Orient the panoramic view on page 41 so it aligns with Mt. Sheridan and the Tetons in the south. The map has already been inverted (with North at the bottom) to assist orientation. The dotted line indicates the approximate rim of the caldera.

A sense of the caldera size can be obtained by using the map to locate these landmarks: Grand Canyon to the southeast, Mt. Sheridan to the south, and the Washburn Range foothills to the west.

The drawing at the top of page 41 shows the panoramic view from Washburn Lookout Station. The numbers indicate five **lines of sight** across the Yellowstone caldera. The numbered lines on the map show the same lines of sight, which are described below.

① Looking across the Grand Canyon of the Yellowstone, where the river cuts through the north caldera rim, to distant volcanic peaks bordering on the eastern rim.

② Looking across the canyon to Lake Yellowstone. The caldera rim bisects the lake from east to west.

③ Looking across the Washburn trail, the canyon, and Hayden Valley to Mt. Sheridan in the Red Mountains, on the south rim of the caldera.

④ Looking across the full length of the caldera to broad plateaus formed by lava that overflowed the southwest rim.

⑤ Looking along the Washburn Range foothills which flank the north rim of the caldera.

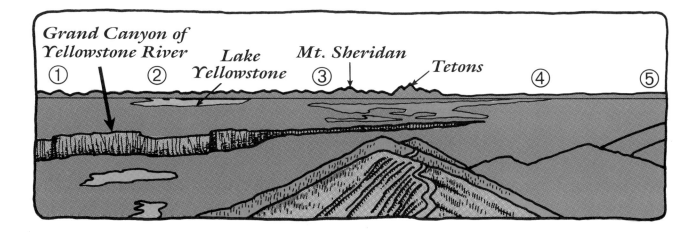

Grand Canyon of Yellowstone River ① ② Lake Yellowstone ③ Mt. Sheridan Tetons ④ ⑤

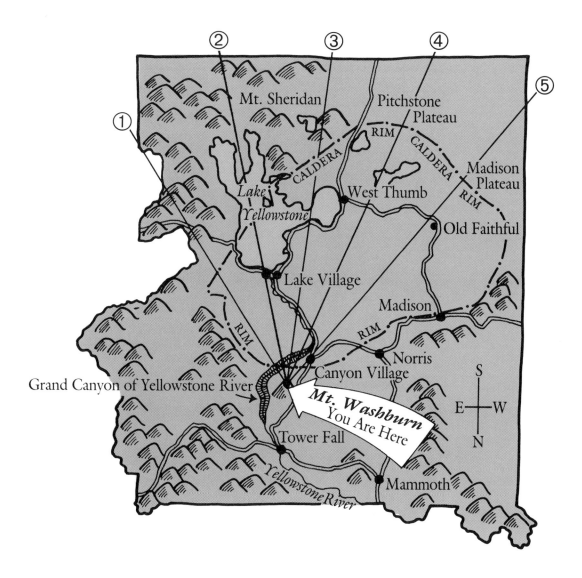

② ③ ④ ⑤

① Mt. Sheridan Pitchstone Plateau

RIM

CALDERA

CALDERA

Lake Yellowstone

West Thumb

Madison Plateau

RIM

Old Faithful

Lake Village

Madison

RIM

RIM

Norris

Grand Canyon of Yellowstone River

Canyon Village

Mt. Washburn
You Are Here

S
E — W
N

Tower Fall

Yellowstone River

Mammoth

Grand Canyon of Yellowstone River *Pelican Cone* ① *Washburn Hot Springs* *Absaroka Range* *Caldera Boundary* *Lake But*

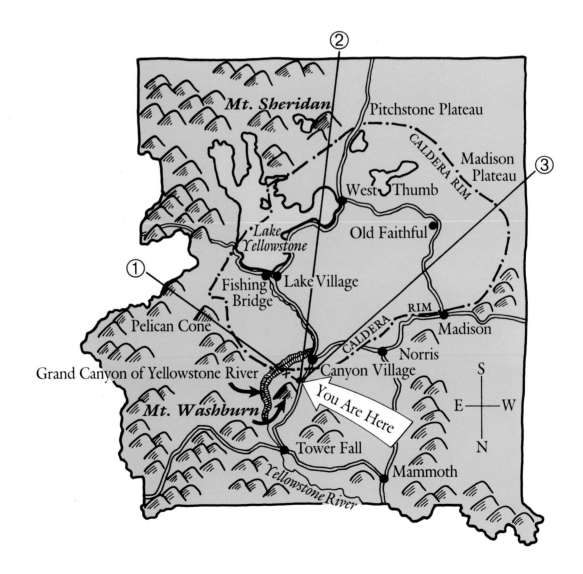

② ③

Mt. Sheridan Pitchstone Plateau

CALDERA RIM

Madison Plateau

West Thumb

Old Faithful

Lake Yellowstone

①

Fishing Bridge

Lake Village

Pelican Cone

RIM

Madison

Grand Canyon of Yellowstone River

CALDERA RIM

Norris

Canyon Village

You Are Here

Mt. Washburn

Tower Fall

Mammoth

Yellowstone River

S E — W N

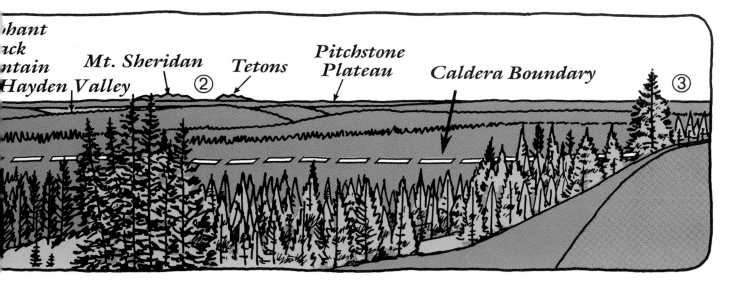

WASHBURN HOT SPRINGS (Caldera Overlook)

The Tetons and Red Mountains in the south are good landmarks for orientation. The dotted line in the panoramic view indicates the approximate rim of the caldera. The top of the map is south. The numbers and numbered lines are:

① Looking east across Washburn Hot Springs and the Grand Canyon of the Yellowstone to a low, forested, round-topped hill called Pelican Cone. This line approximates the northeastern rim of the caldera as it crosses the Grand Canyon of the Yellowstone River.

② Looking south across the barely visible Hayden Valley to Mt. Sheridan in the Red Mountains, on the south rim of the caldera.

③ Looking along the Washburn Range foothills which flank the north rim of the caldera.

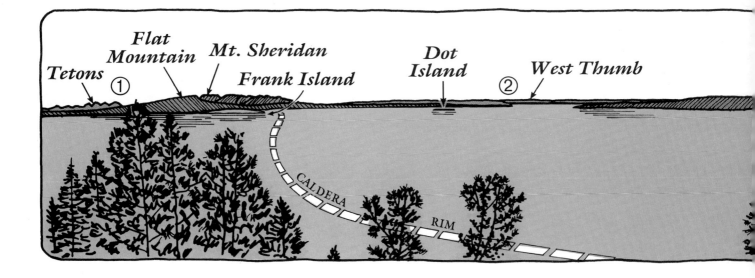

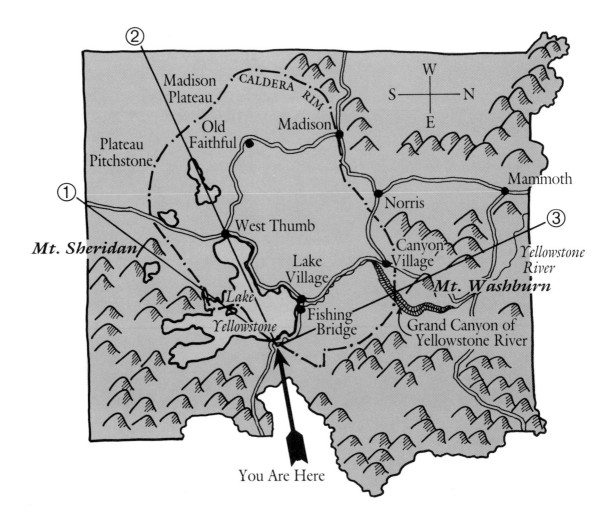

You Are Here

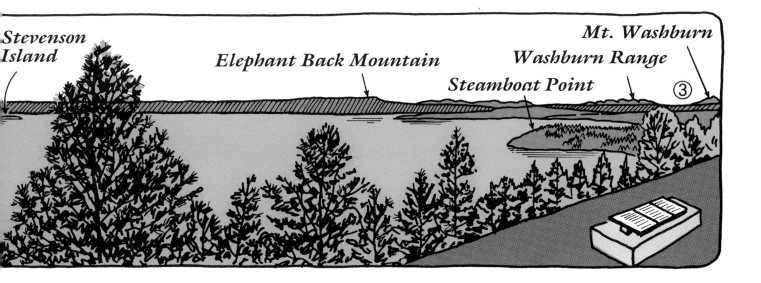

Stevenson Island

Elephant Back Mountain

Steamboat Point

Mt. Washburn

Washburn Range

③

LAKE BUTTE OVERLOOK

The Tetons and Red Mountains to the southwest are good landmarks for orientation. North is to your right, south to the left. The dotted line on the panoramic view shows the approximate rim of the caldera.

① Looking across Frank Island to Mt. Sheridan and the Red Mountains. Flat Mountain and the Tetons are to the left of this line, which follows the southwestern rim of the caldera.

② Looking west across the lake to steamy West Thumb Geyser Basin. The broad plateaus of Pitchstone and Madison fill the horizon, and were formed by overflowing lava from the caldera, whose rim has long since eroded away.

③ Looking across Steamboat Point to Mt. Washburn in the distance. The Washburn Range foothills flank the northern rim.

Numerical Summary of Yellowstone Volcanism

First Period of Volcanism

50,000,000 years ago. Following the creation of the Rocky Mountains, volcanoes erupted for 10,000,000 years, building a thick layer of volcanic material and burying many forests, which petrified. The volcanic mountain ranges of Washburn and Absaroka were formed.

Second Period of Volcanism

2,000,000 years ago. The first of three eruptive cycles reached its peak of volcanic activity, and subsequently poured 600 cubic miles of magma onto Yellowstone plateau, producing a caldera which has been largely obliterated by erosion and later volcanic cycles.

1,200,000 years ago. The second eruptive cycle reached its activity peak and produced 67 cubic miles of plateau magma.

600,000 years ago. The third cycle reached its peak and 240 cubic miles of magma poured from the subsurface magma chamber. The chamber roof collapsed cataclysmically, forming a caldera 47 miles long and 28 miles wide. The caldera refilled with lava flows and the caldera floor domed over the refilling magma chamber.

150,000 years ago a small caldera formed in the area of West Thumb.

70,000 years ago the last lava flowed in Yellowstone, forming the Pitchstone Plateau.

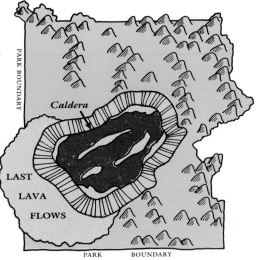

GLOSSARY

CALDERA—A large cup- or basin-shaped crater, caused by inward collapse of a volcano after eruption.

CONTINENT—A slab of rock that forms a large (named) land mass, like the North American Continent. Continents are generally above sea level except at their margins, and are composed of granitic rock.

CONVECTION—A circular, vertical movement of a fluid medium caused by heating from below. Hotter, therefore less dense, material rises; cooler, heavier material sinks. A convection current refers to the path taken by the liquid medium as it rises after being heated, and falls after cooling.

CORE—The deep interior of the earth; composed of iron and nickel.

CRUST—The cooled, rocky layer that floats on the mantle. Crust may be continental or oceanic depending on its location and density. Crust and lithosphere are used synonymously. Continental crust is composed primarily of granite. Oceanic crust is composed of basalt.

EROSION—The group of processes whereby earthy or rock material is loosened or dissolved and removed from any part of the earth's surface.

FUMAROLE—A thermal feature that forms where there is a boiling water table, but too little water to make a hot spring or geyser. It is a vent producing mainly steam.

GEOTHERMAL—Of or pertaining to the heat of the earth's interior.

GEYSER—A column of steam and water that periodically shoots out of the ground under pressure from the heating water at depth.

HOT SPOT—A persistent, stationary source of thermal activity which remains anchored in the deep mantle while the plates of crust pass over it. Magmas heated by the hot spot rise to the surface in plumes. Hot spots are millions of years old.

LAVA—Magma that flows out of a volcano onto the surface of the earth.

MAGMA—Liquid or molten rock beneath the surface of the earth.

MANTLE—The layer beneath the crust.

PANGAEA—An ancient super-continent that contained virtually all the earth's continental crust.

PLATE—A very large piece of crust given a name like North American plate, Eurasian plate, or African plate. A plate of crust generally consists of continental crust, oceanic crust, or mixtures of both.

PLUME—The theoretical conduit of heat from the mantle to crust. The plume appears to be composed of quasi-liquid rock streaming upward from a hot spot anchored in the deep mantle.

RIFT—A crack in the earth's crust through which magma pours out, forming new crust. Cracks or rifts may occur in crusts of ocean or continent.

SEA-FLOOR SPREADING—The theory that ocean floor is created by the rifting and separation of crustal plates along mid-ocean ridges, with new ocean crust formed from magma rising out of the mantle to fill the rift.

VOLCANISM—Volcanic power or activity. The term ordinarily includes all natural processes resulting in the formation of volcanoes, volcanic rocks, lava flows, etc.

RECOMMENDED READING

Dunning, F. W., P. J. Adams, J. C. Thackray, S. van Rose, I. F. Mercer, and R. H. Roberts. *The Story of the Earth*. London: Geological Museum, Institute of Geological Sciences, 1981.

Fiero, Bill. *Geology of the the Great Basin*. Reno: University of Nevada Press, 1986.

Fritz, William J. *Roadside Geology of the Yellowstone Country*. Missoula: Mountain Press, 1985.

Gore, Rick. "Our Restless Planet Earth," *National Geographic*. August 1985, pp 142–181.

Keefer, William R. *The Geologic Story of Yellowstone National Park*. Yellowstone: Yellowstone Library and Museum Association, 1984.

Love, J. D. and John C. Reed, Jr. *Creation of the Teton Landscape*. Moose, WY: Grand Teton Natural History Association, 1979.

"Volcanoes and the Earth's Interior," *Scientific American*. San Francisco: W. H. Freeman, 1982.

ABOUT THE AUTHOR

William H. Cottrell grew up in the midwest, a bit east of Kansas City, Missouri. Colorado State University granted him a B.S. in Zoology prior to attending medical school at the University of Missouri. Military experience in Alaska preceded an orthopaedic surgical residency at the University of Southern California. He now lives with his family in Placerville, California, where he is engaged in the private practice of orthopaedic surgery. Mountains and rock-climbing consume his avocational time. He is one of those many self-appointed inspectors of Yellowstone.